What Makes a Bug a Bug?

A Bucky and Bingo Learning Adventure

Andi Cann

I hope you enjoy learning about bugs today! Please visit my website https://www.andicann.com and register your email address. You will receive a free book and be the first to know about new books, special offers, and free stuff!

If you have a chance, please write a review. It helps other readers and me, an independent author. Thank you!

Andi

A note to parents.

Kids love exploring nature! They especially love the creepy, crawly, fascinating world of bugs. For the purposes of this book, the word bug and insect are used interchangeably. However, bugs are technically a subset of insects.

Insects are the most diverse class of animals. There are more insect species than any other group with more than 900,000 types of insects. But how do you explain the difference between a spider (arachnid) and a bee (insect)? Or a snail (gastropoda) and a praying mantis (insect)? What exactly makes a bug a bug? Join Bucky and Bingo as they learn about the concept of "animal class." Insects are members of the Insecta or Hexapoda class (made up of segmented bodies, jointed legs and external skeletons.) Bugs' primary differentiator is that they have six legs, three body parts, and two antennae. Some have wings when they reach the adult stage. There are other arthropods (like spiders) that are small, crawl, and are generally thought to be insects, but they're not! Have fun exploring science with your children!

For all parents who support their children's love of reading
and bugs!

Hi! I'm Bucky. This is Bingo. Today I asked my parents about the creeping, crawling, flying things around the house and in our yard.

They asked, do you mean...BUGS?

I guess so. What makes a bug a bug? Is a spider a bug? Is a turtle a bug? What about worms? Are they bugs?

We read the magic mystery book, and it led us on a journey.

First, we looked in the dirt. There were lots of worms! Are they bugs? They look like bugs.

Then, we looked at a flower. I spy a lady bug. It has "bug" in its name. I guess it's a bug.

We looked at our horse. She had flies all around her. Is a fly a bug? I DO know a horse isn't a bug!

The book said that you can detect a bug by looking at its body. They

have

a

6.3.2

body.

What is that?

We read a
little bit more.
For a bug to
be a bug, it
must have six
legs. This
beetle has six
legs. It must be a bug!

But is that all? No! The book also says that a bug must have three parts to its body. A velvet ant

has 6 legs AND 3 parts to its body. It also must be a bug.

Finally, the book says a bug must have two antennae, the funny things that stick out of its head.

This praying mantis has six legs, 3 parts to its body, AND 2 antennae. Yea! Now, we know it's a bug!

So, the rule for checking out little creatures is to see if they have 6.3.2. What do you think about that, Bingo?

Bugs are so small. How do I know if they have six legs, three body parts, and two antennae?

First, collect some bugs. BUT, ask your mom or dad to help you. Some bugs bite or sting! Ouch!

When you find a bug, put it into a small clear plastic cup. But, don't leave the bug in the cup for very long!

Let's collect a few bugs! We have to be careful

not to step on them!

Here's an ant. Let's see if it's a bug! Yes! Six legs, three body parts, and two antennae. It's a bug!

What about these creatures?

Nope. Not enough feet!

Here's a spider. Is it a bug? The spider has eight legs, only two body parts and no antennae. I thought spiders were bugs but they're not!

We checked a butterfly
and some bees. 6.3.2.

Yep. All
bugs.

Then, we checked out a worm and a caterpillar. Nope! Too many feet or not enough!

Then, we checked out a snail. Not a bug. Did you know some people eat snails? EWWW!

What Bingo? Are you a bug?
Nooooo! You're not a bug. You
only have four feet. Which is
why…

The turtle is definitely NOT a bug!
Can you imagine a tortoise with

six

legs?

That

would

be

funny!

The book says that a tortoise (or turtle) is an amphibian Weird! Hmmm, I wonder what makes an animal an AM. FIB. IAN?

Bingo, we learned what makes a bug a bug!

We know that some bugs sing,

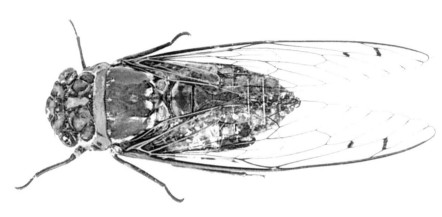

others sting.

Some eat flower dust, others eat poo.

But now you know, a bug is a bug if its body has 6.3.2.

ALWAYS get your parents to help you with bugs because some of them sting! Ouch!

Bugs, in order of appearance:

There are many other books by <u>Andi Cann</u>. Check them out at your favorite book seller!

Published by MindView Press: Hibou

ISBN-13:   978-1-949761-15-3   eBook

ISBN-13:   978-1-949761-16-0   Paperback

Thank you for reading!

40519826R00022

Made in the USA
Middletown, DE
27 March 2019